Poetry Parties
∘ FOR LITTLES ∘

Insects and Spiders

© 2021 Jenny Phillips | goodandbeautiful.com

Poetry Parties

∘ FOR LITTLES ∘

Insects and Spiders

Written by The Good and the Beautiful Team
Special thanks to Shannen Yauger, Project Director

Illustrations by Mackenzie Rose West
Designed by Phillip Colhouer
Cover design by Robin Fight

A Note to Parents

Why Poetry Parties?

Poetry is the language of the imagination. Poetry teaches a child, often in a fun, rhyming way, to express emotion. It inspires a child to laugh, and what better way for a young child to learn than through a fun time with his or her parent?

Poetry Parties for Littles is a simple guide to planning a special time of celebrating poetry and nature with your preschool-age child. Each themed party is laid out carefully and includes poetry, supply lists, and crafts with photographs and directions so that you can enjoy the party as much as your little one!

About this Book

This book is broken up into the following sections:

* Ladybugs and Fireflies
* Spiders and Flies
* Up in the Sky: Bees, Dragonflies, and Butterflies
* Down on the Ground: Ants, Grasshoppers, Caterpillars, and Other Insects That Crawl

Each section has poetry to share with your child, activities that go along with the poetry, and crafts. Follow the instructions in the blue bubbles, read the poems aloud, and create the crafts. It is up to you to decide how much to do in each section. The most important thing is to enjoy this time with your child.

Party Guide

The Party

Each section can be hosted as one long party or broken into smaller parties. Each craft is set up to be completed by one child or multiple children. The supplies listed are per child.

We encourage you to complete the outdoor activities that appear throughout this party guide. Experiencing nature allows children to make a personal connection with what they are learning through play.

Party Preparation

1. Read through the "Supplies Needed" section and gather any supplies that you do not have at home.

2. Read through the "Additional Party Decorations" section and decide which decorations you want to use.

3. Decorate for the party and do the preparation section for each activity or craft.

4. Follow the instructions for the party in the blue bubbles that appear throughout this guide.

Ladybugs and Fireflies

SUPPLIES NEEDED

✓ REMEMBER   You don't need to do all the crafts, activities, or decorations.

Ladybug Puppet (p. 9)

* black and red construction paper
* black washable paint
* googly eyes
* white string
* white chalk marker
* paper plate

Ladybug Fruit Cookies (p. 10)

* cream cheese
* round cookies
* strawberries
* blueberries

Firefly Suncatcher (p. 14)

* yellow, green, and white washable paint
* black construction paper
* tracing paper
* googly eyes (optional)

Markers, scissors, hole punch, tape, standard white paper, ruler, and glue should always be on hand and are not listed in the "Supplies Needed" sections.

Additional Party Decorations

Ladybug Decorations

* Blow up red balloons and color black dots on them for the ladybugs.
* Using a permanent marker, color red napkins with black dots.
* Sprinkle black circles from a hole punch on a red tablecloth (or black and red dots on a white tablecloth).
* Color black dots on red plastic cups for drinks.

Firefly Decorations

* Blow up yellow balloons and draw black wings on them for the fireflies.
* Using a permanent marker, color yellow napkins with black wings.
* Sprinkle black circles from a hole punch on a yellow tablecloth.
* Color black wings on yellow plastic cups for drinks.

Decorate your table with little mason jars of flowers, twigs, leaves, or grass.

BRING THE OUTSIDE IN!

Poetry Time!

Silently read the text in this circle and then read the poem on this page aloud to the children while they are in a yard/park, looking outside the window at a yard/park, or looking at a picture of a yard/park.

Bugs in My Backyard

Jenny Phillips and Shannen Yauger

Oh, how beautiful it is to see,

A spotted ladybug on my tree,

A yellow bee on a flower white,

A firefly shining in the night,

A grasshopper green on golden wheat,

A line of ants marching on the street,

A dragonfly zooming all around,

A butterfly flitting without a sound.

Ladybug

Unknown

The ladybug's a beetle.
It's shaped like a pea.
Its color is a bright red
With lots of spots to see.

You Are Welcome, Ladybug

Jenny Phillips and Maggie Felsch

You are welcome in my garden,
Ladybug so red.
I love your black polka dots
and your little black head.
You are welcome in my garden
to climb as you please
on the flowers and pumpkins,
tomatoes and trees.
You are welcome in my garden
as my special guest.
When God the Father made you,
the whole world was blessed.

Ladybug, Ladybug

Ivy O. Eastwick

Ladybug, Ladybug,
Where do you hide?

Under a leaf on its feathery side;
Safe from the lightning—
And safe from the rain—
Here I shall stay till
The sun shines again.

Ladybug Puppet

1. Start by cutting out all the pieces you'll need for your ladybug finger puppet. You will need two large black circles (one slightly smaller than the other) and one large red circle cut in half.

2. Cut two holes at the bottom of the larger black circle. These holes should be big enough for your child's fingers to fit inside of them.

3. Glue the red circle halves onto the large black circle that has finger holes. Glue the red halves at an angle, leaving an opening for the holes. These are the wings. Then glue the smaller black circle on top for the ladybug's head.

4. Fold your white string into a V and glue it onto the back of the ladybug's head for the antennae. Then glue on your googly eyes and draw a cute smile on your ladybug with your white chalk marker.

5. Finish your adorable ladybug finger puppet by pouring a small amount of black paint onto a paper plate. Dip your finger into the paint and then onto your ladybug's wings to make spots.

Complete any of the crafts, games, and activities that you desire in this section.

Ladybug Fruit Cookies

* Spread cream cheese on the cookies in a thin layer.
* Slice the strawberries in half and set each half on the lower half of a cookie, like open wings.
* Place a blueberry above the strawberry for the head.

Children love to wiggle! Read the poem on this page and encourage your child to act out the poem.

Fireflies, Fireflies

Shannen Yauger

Fireflies, fireflies
By the tree.
How many children
Do you see?

Fireflies, fireflies
In the sky.
See all the children
Jump so high!

Fireflies, fireflies
Near the ground.
With so many children
Running around!

Fireflies, fireflies
In the night.
Now all the children
Are out of sight.

Firefly

Elizabeth Madox Roberts

A little light is going by,
Is going up to see the sky,
A little light with wings.

I never could have thought of it,
To have a little bug all lit
And made to go on wings.

Glow, Firefly, Glow

Sue Stuever Battel

I'm a shining firefly;
Watch me glow.
Soon my flitting friends and I
Will all light up a show.

On a summer evening,
Look out on the lawn.
You will find us signaling
As we flash lights off and on.

Firefly Suncatcher

* Cut two ovals, about three inches in length, from the black construction paper. You will also need to cut one circle for the firefly's head and two small strips for the antennae.

* Cut a large oval out of the white tracing paper. Have your child dip his or her finger in the yellow paint and then the green paint and make dots that cover the oval.

* Let this dry, then glue the pieces together as shown. Add googly eyes or make small fingerprint eyes with white paint.

Additional Activities

* Glow stick dance! Give your child glow sticks and turn on some fun music. Have him or her dance around the room. This is fun to do in the evening in the yard as well!

* Purchase a ladybug kit online. Have a ladybug release party when they are fully developed.

* Make ladybug and firefly "pets" out of balloons. Let the children hit them in the air so that they do not touch the ground.

Spiders and Flies

SUPPLIES NEEDED

✔ REMEMBER **You don't need to do all the crafts, activities, or decorations.**

Spider Hat (p. 25)

* 3 pieces of black construction paper
* white washable paint
* any color bright washable paint

Spider Crackers (p. 26)

* round crackers (2 per spider)
* cream cheese
* pretzel sticks (4 per spider)
* olives or blueberries
* knife

Markers, scissors, hole punch, tape, standard white paper, ruler, and glue should always be on hand and are not listed in the "Supplies Needed" sections.

Additional Party Decorations

Spider Decorations

* Blow up black balloons and tape crinkled legs on them.

* Hang white streamers in a spider web pattern across the windows or in the corner of the room.

Fly Decorations

* Blow up brown balloons and tape construction paper wings on them like a fly.

* Make paper fly swatters using straws and construction paper and set at each place setting.

Swish Away That Fly!

Shannen Yauger

Swish your tail, big brown cow;
That is what you are supposed to do
When the itty-bitty stinging fly
Comes too close to you!

The Zooming Fly!

Jenny Phillips

Almost quicker than my eye can see,
A fly zooms back and forth by me.
Two thin wings beat fast, it's true—
Three hundred times before I count to two.
That is what makes the buzzing sound
As the fly goes round and round.
Flying up, backwards, and side to side,
Wouldn't it be fun to ride on a fly?

The Fly

Theodore Tilton

Baby Bye,

Here's a fly:

Let us watch him, you and I.

How he crawls

Up the walls—

Yet he never falls!

I believe, with those six legs,

You and I could walk on eggs!

There he goes,

On his toes,

Tickling Baby's nose!

Spots of red

Dot his head;

Rainbows on his wings are
spread!

That small speck

Is his neck;

See him nod and beck!

I can show you, if you choose,

Where to look to find his shoes:

Three small pairs

Made of hairs—

These he always wears.

Is a Spider an Insect?

Jenny Phillips

Is a spider an insect?

No, a spider is an arachnid.

Arachnid, arachnid?

That's a big word for a little kid!

I'll just call it a crawly, smart thing

That weaves silver webs

And doesn't have wings,

A clever creature with eight legs

That knows how to lay hundreds of eggs!

Spiders

Unknown

Clever spider spins a thread

To make a trap we call a web.

Clever spider knows that she

Will have some insects with her tea.

The Scurrying Spider

Alicia Scott

Oh, how it scurries, scuttles, and scoots,

I watch as the spider climbs over my boot.

I wonder if eight legs would let me run so fast?

As the brown little creature disappears into

the grass.

Black Widow

Alicia Scott

With shiny black body

And hourglass red,

She lays hundreds of eggs,

A papery sac for their bed.

Her silken, tangled web

Lies low to the ground,

While she waits for her prey,

Hanging upside down.

The Itsy Bitsy Spider

Unknown

The itsy bitsy spider climbed up
the waterspout.
Down came the rain
and washed the spider out.
Out came the sun
and dried up all the rain,
and the itsy bitsy spider climbed
up the spout again.

Spider, Spider

Amy Drorbaugh

Spider, spider spin your web,
Spinning silk, your shining thread.
Glisten, glisten in the sun,
Hanging lace, your job is done.

The Spider

Lucy Spooner

Behold the spider in his cell!

How cunningly he weaves!

He sometimes makes his silky nest

Close in among the leaves.

Sometimes he spreads his airy tent

Upon the velvet grass,

Where through a pretty central door

He in and out can pass.

The Spider Web

Shannen Yauger

I just walked through a spider web;

The strands I did not see.

It was meant to catch bugs, I'm sure,

But instead it caught me!

Spider Eyes

Amy Drorbaugh

Oh, what can you see, with your eight
tiny eyes
When you look at the world, the earth,
and the skies?
Do your eight eyes make things look
bigger or brighter to you?
It doesn't seem fair that I only have two.

Spider Hat Craft

* Cut a strip of black construction paper about one inch wide, long enough to wrap around your child's head. You may need to tape two pieces of paper together to make it long enough. Tape the ends together to form a circle.

* Cut eight strips of black paper, each about a half-inch wide and the length of a piece of construction paper (9 inches).

* Fold the eight strips of paper in a fan fold to make them "crinkle" (see image for example). These will be the spider's legs.

* Tape the legs to the circle, four on either side.

* Dip the child's thumb into white paint, and make two dots in the middle of the circle for eyes. Optional: Dip the child's pinky finger in colored paint to make the middle of the eyes.

Spider Crackers

* Spread cream cheese on the crackers in a thin layer.

* Place two crackers together to form a sandwich.

* Break four pretzel sticks in half, then wedge four halves into the cream cheese filling on both sides of the sandwiched crackers.

* Put two small dabs of cream cheese on the top cracker. These are the bases for the eyes.

* Place one blueberry on each cream cheese dab to make the eyes. Optional: Instead of blueberries, slice an olive in half, placing one half on each cream cheese dab.

Additional Activities

* Create a spider web with string, spanning a door frame. The children can try to crawl through it without breaking it.
* Use the fly swatter decorations and have the children "swat" flies in this book.

Bees, Dragonflies, and Butterflies

✔ REMEMBER You don't need to do all the crafts, activities, or decorations.

Bumblebee Puppet (p. 33)

* yellow construction paper
* popsicle sticks
* black yarn (or black
  construction paper)
* googly eyes

Butterfly Cinnamon Toast (p. 37)

* I slice of bread per child
* butter
* cinnamon
* I banana per child
* knife
* optional: toothpicks and
  blueberries

Markers, scissors, hole punch, tape, standard white paper, ruler, and glue should always be on hand and are not listed in the "Supplies Needed" sections.

Additional Party Decorations

Bee Decorations

* Decorate with yellow flowers and honeycomb-shaped cereal.

* Blow up yellow balloons and paint black stripes on them to make bumblebees.

* Use the bumblebee puppet craft on page 33 as place holders.

The Song of a Bee

Marian Douglas

BUZZ-z-z-z-z-z, buzz!

This is the song of the bee;

His legs are of yellow,

A jolly good fellow,

And yet a great worker is he.

I'm a Little Honeybee

Unknown
(to the tune of "I'm a Little Tea Pot")

I'm a little honeybee,

Yellow and black.

See me gather

Pollen on my back.

What the queen bee tells me,

I must do

So I can make sweet honey for you!

Do You Like to Buzz?

Unknown
(to the tune of "Do Your Ears Hang Low?")

Do you like to buzz?

Are you covered all in fuzz?

Do you call a hive a home

In the garden where you roam?

Do you know how to make honey?

Are your stripes a little funny?

Do you like to buzz?

The Swarm of Bees

Elsa Gorham Baker

One little honeybee by my window flew;

Soon came another—then there were two.

Two happy honeybees in the apple tree;

One more bee came buzzing up—then there were three.

Three busy honeybees starting to explore

Another bee came to help—then there were four.

Four laden honeybees flying to the hive;

They were joined by one more bee—then there were five.

Five tired honeybees with the others mix;

Now there's a swarm of them—a hundred times six.

Honeybee on My Nose

Maggie Felsch

I saw a honeybee one day,

flying all about,

And when she buzzed around my head,

I didn't run or shout.

I watched her as she slowed her wings

and landed on my nose!

How glad I felt that a honeybee

mistook me for a rose.

Bumblebee Puppet

* Cut one small circle and one medium circle out of yellow construction paper.
* Glue these on the popsicle stick as shown.
* Cut 6–10 pieces of black yarn (black construction paper can be used if you do not have yarn).
* Glue these pieces across the yellow circles, then trim to fit.
* Glue googly eyes to the head of the bee, and use small strips of yarn (or paper) for the antennae.

I started as a tiny egg
Upon a leaf of green.
Unless you look very closely,
My eggs cannot be seen.

Butterfly Life Cycle

Jenny Phillips

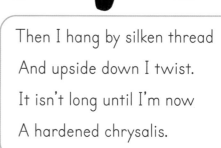

I hatch into a caterpillar
And slowly, slowly crawl.
I munch and munch
And eat and eat
The nice leaves big and small.

Then I hang by silken thread
And upside down I twist.
It isn't long until I'm now
A hardened chrysalis.

And now I stretch my pretty wings,
So colorful and bright.
I go to see this big, wide world
And soon fly out of sight.

You cannot see what's happening,
It might seem very strange.
I will come out a butterfly
After my mighty change.

Children love to dance and act! Have your children act out the poem, starting out as if they are hiding, then curling into a ball, standing with their head toward the ground, then stretching their arms wide, and finally flying away.

Mr. Butterfly

Unknown

Butterfly, butterfly, where do you fly?

Where do you go alone?

Is it for flowers and honey you spy?

Have you a home of your own?

What is your name?

Do you live in the wood?

And what do you come to see?

Dear Mr. Butterfly, won't you tell

Your secrets to someone like me?

The Butterfly and the Kitten

Shannen Yauger

My kitten watched a butterfly

Land upon the rose.

Then my kitten was surprised

When it landed on his nose!

Butterfly
Cinnamon Toast

* Toast a slice of bread, and then spread a bit of butter and sprinkle cinnamon on it.
* Cut the bread in half diagonally to form two triangles.
* Slice a banana in half lengthwise to use as the body.
* Set the toast on either side of the banana.
* Optional: Use short toothpicks to hold blueberries on the banana for the eyes.

A Dragonfly

Eleanor Farjeon

When the heat of the summer
Made drowsy the land,
A dragonfly came
And sat on my hand.
With its blue jointed body,
And wings like spun glass,
It lit on my fingers
As though they were grass.

The Dazzling Dragonfly

Rebecca Borger

Dragonfly zooming by,
Flying backwards through the sky.
Brilliant blue or emerald green,
Reflecting golden sun's bright beams.
Fierce as fire, fast as light,
Dazzling everyone with its flight.

Additional Activities

* Have your child make up dances to the poems on pages 30 and 31.

* Have your child pretend to be a dragonfly and "fly" around the room to different places that you call out. Remember that a dragonfly's wings always flap!

* Take a nature walk and try to find bumblebees, butterflies, and dragonflies.

Down on the Ground:
Ants, Grasshoppers, Caterpillars, and Other Insects That Crawl

✔ REMEMBER **You don't need to do all the crafts, activities, or decorations.**

Ants on My Pants Game (p. 45)

* white construction paper
* black washable paint
* double-sided tape
* a pair of the child's pants
* a blindfold

Cricket Hat (p. 48)

* green construction paper
* white construction paper
* black crayon

Markers, scissors, hole punch, tape, standard white paper, ruler, and glue should always be on hand and are not listed in the "Supplies Needed" sections.

Additional Party Decorations

Bug Decorations

* Blow up black balloons, and add paper legs on them. Place them on the table and on the ground as if they are ants crawling. Optional: You can tape the ant balloons to the walls or windows as if they are crawling all over the room.

* Add paper heads to black paper plates to look like beetles.

* Set gummy worms around the table to appear to be crawling out of the decorations.

Grasshopper on the Garden Wall

Shannen Yauger

I saw a green grasshopper
Jump high on the garden wall.
Look out, green grasshopper,
That wall is oh-so-tall!

Grasshopper

Unknown

Hop, Hop, Hop,
My, what strength.
A grasshopper hops
Twenty times its length.
Hop in the grass
Or on a single blade.
Hop in the sun
Or hop in the shade.
Farmer says, "Grasshopper,
Stay off my crop!"
There goes the grasshopper,
HOP, HOP, HOP!

Beetles

Shannen Yauger

One beetle, two beetles,
three beetles, four.
Scuttle, scuttle, quick look!
Here comes one more.

Five shiny green beetles
Walking in a row.
Scuttle, scuttle, quick look!
Oh, where did they all go?

The Dance of the Ants

Amy Drorbaugh

I lie in the grass, with my head in my hand,
And watch you go by one by one.
Marching to the beat of your own silent band,
Your line stays so straight while you run.

Then into the hill, you each disappear,
You carry your bounty back home.
Once safe inside you have nothing to fear;
The work of the day is now done.

Ants on My Pants Game

Set up:

* Cut out five to six 3-inch squares from white construction paper.

* Have the child dip his or her thumb in the washable black paint and make three dots in a line.

* Once the paint is dry, draw legs, antennae, and eyes on your ant. There should now be one ant on each piece of paper you cut out.

* Hang a pair of the child's pants on a wall or set them on a sofa as if they are standing up.

* Place double-sided tape on the back of each ant.

To play the game:

* Using a safe item of your choice, blindfold each child on his or her turn.

* One at a time, have each child try to place all the ants on one leg of the pants in a line from bottom to top.

* The "winner" of the game is the child who places the ants in the straightest line.

The Caterpillar

Christina Rossetti

Brown and furry
Caterpillar in a hurry;
Take your walk
To the shady leaf or stalk.
May no toad spy you,
May the little birds pass by you;
Spin and die,
To live again a butterfly.

Fuzzy Wuzzy Caterpillar

Unknown

Fuzzy wuzzy caterpillar
 in the garden creeps.
He spins himself a blanket
 and soon falls fast asleep.

Fuzzy wuzzy caterpillar
 wakes up by and by.
To find he has wings of beauty,
 changed to a butterfly.

Inch-Worm

Dorothy Aldis

Little green inch-worm,

Inch-worm, inch.

You can't hurt me;

You don't pinch.

Never did anyone

Any harm

So take your little green walk

Up my arm.

Inchworms are not really worms! They are caterpillars that look odd when they move because they have legs at both ends of their bodies.

Cricket

Maggie Felsch

Little black cricket

Hides in the thicket,

Playing his lullaby song.

Soon my eyes close,

My mind starts to doze,

And he plays for me all night long.

Cricket Hat

* Cut a strip of green construction paper about one inch wide, long enough to wrap around your child's head. You may need to tape two pieces of paper together to make it long enough. Tape the ends together to form a circle.

* Cut eight strips of green paper, each about a half-inch wide and the length of a piece of construction paper (9 inches).

* Fold the strips of paper in a fan fold to make them "crinkle" (see image for example).

* Tape the crinkled strips to the circle, three on either side. These are the cricket's legs.

* Cut two circles of green paper, then two circles of white paper. The white circles should be half the size of the green. These are the cricket's eyes.

* Glue the white circles onto the green.

* Use the black crayon to color in eyeballs.

* Glue or tape these eyes to the band that goes around the child's head.

* Tape the remaining two crinkled strips behind the eyes. These are the antennae.

Additional Activities

* Tell your child to act like an ant for 10 minutes. Your child must crawl everywhere he or she goes.

* Tell your child to act like a cricket for 10 minutes. Your child must jump on all fours everywhere he or she goes.

* Tell your child to act like an inchworm for 10 minutes. Your child must "inch" everywhere he or she goes.

* Discuss what your child discovered about being this low to the ground.